100 POEMS FOR 100 PEOPLE

Although each individual poem is dedicated to someone very special,
I would also like to dedicate every word to every person who finds
this book in their hands.My hope is that you will feel the magical
inspiration, upliftment and love that I weaved into my poems just for
YOU.

100 Poems for 100 People

ISBN: 978-1-910181-36-2

First edition published in November 2016

Published in Great Britain by the Anchor Print Group Ltd

THE LITTLE GNOME

A flash of red amongst the green,
The little gnome goes about his work unseen,
Loving the stones and making them gleam,
Polishing crystals in the bubbling stream,
Talking to the rocks and singing to the birds,
Making the soil fertile, with his magic words.
When all is still come dusky night,
The little gnome with his eyes ever so bright,
Charts the stars in the heavens above,
And sends all the celestial beings his love ...

For Ashley Kavanagh

A BIT OF WINTER MAGIC

Early this morning while all were asleep,

I ventured into the garden to take a little peep,

At the work of Jack Frost who'd paid a visit in the night,

Leaving his ice patterns gleaming in the light,

There were baubles of ice hanging on the fir trees,

A cobweb necklace for the fairies, draped on the berries,

The Winter may often be dreary and cold,

But when Jack Frost has been what a sight to behold,

There's always beauty to be found in Nature you see,

No matter what season it may happen to be,

Let the work of Nature lift your Spirit and your Soul,

And the fairies make you feel magical, happy and whole

For Katherine Miles

THE BEST MEDICINE IS LOVE

Little Bear lay in bed feeling down in the dumps,

He had a very sore throat and a case of the grumps,

Then Mummy Bear came in with a bottle and a spoon,

Ohhhhh Little Bear cried, it's medicine time again so soon??

But Mummy Bear just smiled, and put down the tray,

Little Bear she said, I have something to say,

There's no medicine in the bottle, but the bottle is still full,

Little Bear was puzzled and a frowny face he began to pull,

The best medicine I can give you, Mummy Bear began to smile

Is a bottle full of my love, it works better by a mile,

Now come and have a snuggle, Mummy Bear said,

Know how much I love you, while you're lying in your bed,

And always and forever my heart will fit you like a glove,

For the best medicine in the world is a bottle full of LOVE!

For Patricia Clanzy-Hodge

SENDING SNUGGLES...

Sending snuggles and cuddles, and warm comforting hugs

Hot soups and hot chocolates in big steaming mugs

On these cold and damp Autumn days

I wish you the sunshine's golden rays

To uplift and warm the coldest of hearts

For the heart within is where it all starts

It matters not how cold it is outside

When you feel all warm and fuzzy inside

So go out today and share a warming hug or two

And put LOVE into all you say and do...

For Helena Van-Moll

SOMEWHERE CLOSE TO HEAVEN

Somewhere close to Heaven, in a place called Fairyland,

A little elf knelt on one knee and took a fairy by the hand,

Fairy I love you more than all the stars up in the sky,

You're the one who gave me wings so that I could fly,

When I think of you my heart soars and reaches Heavens heights,

My love for you, please imagine, glows like a million fairy lights,

I've known you for a thousand years and now it's time to say,

Fairy you are in my heart and mind every second of the day,

Please be mine and I will love you til the sunbeams are no more,

Let us fly over the rainbow, and together our hearts will soar.

For Paul Kavanagh

THE FRIEND I'VE NEVER MET

Somewhere in the world out there,

And you will know just who you are,

Is a special person who I have come to know,

Who I talk to from afar,

Even though we have never met,

You are always there for me,

To listen, to laugh and share all things,

And love me unconditionally,

I am very blessed to have you,

And you I won't forget,

The precious gift of you out there, the friend I've never met ...

For Deidre Byrne

A MUM IS A SPECIAL GIFT

A Mum is a special gift from above,

Who wraps you up in a blanket of love,

She tells you that it will all be ok,

She always knows the right words to say,

Mums are precious, Mums are unique,

They're a light shining bright, when all's looking bleak,

A little slice of Heaven is my Mum to me,

My Mum made me all I grew up to be....

For Doreen Lucas

WHEN ONE DOOR CLOSES

When one door closes and you're in despair,

When your dreams have been shattered and it doesn't seem fair,

Always remember that there's a bigger better door,

The one you've really been waiting for,

It may seem that you haven't got your way,

But you're needed elsewhere, so come what may,

That old door wasn't really right for you,

There is something bigger and much better for you to do,

In the long run it will benefit you more,

So take comfort in my words for of this I am sure,

If you take a leap of faith and just wait,

All will be well, it's a matter of fate,

Close the door and soon you will see,

A shining new door, full of possibilities...

For Jacky Fowler

BENEATH THE SEA

Beneath the sea there's another world,

Where the Merfolk dwell,

They play amongst the shells and rocks,

And have many stories to tell,

About how with the whales and dolphins,

They are the guardians of the sea,

They take care of all the sea creatures,

And keep the water as clean as it can be,

If you visit the ocean,

You might be lucky to catch a glimpse,

Of a flash of golden mermaid hair,

Or the tail of one of these sea imps,

Next time you're at the seaside,

Put a shell up to your ear,

Can you hear the Merfolk calling?

Their voices can you hear?

They call to us to help them,

Put our love back into the sea,

To stop polluting the oceans,

And keep them flowing naturally.

For Ilan Shahor

I BELIEVE IN YOU

Don't let them tell you, you can't do it,

Don't let them tell you that you're wrong,

Don't believe that you're no good,

You must sing your own sweet song,

Don't let them tell you will fail,

Don't worry if you're misunderstood,

Don't let them tell you it's a waste of time,

Don't be stuck in the mud,

BELIEVE that you can do it

BELIEVE that you are right,

BELIEVE you're full of goodness,

Let your own sweet song shine out so bright,

BELIEVE that all things are possible,

BELIEVE that dreams come true,

BELIEVE that it will all be worthwhile,

Because I believe in YOU!

For Luke Lishman

CHANGE

Change can be an unwelcome part of life,

But I want you to know,

It helps to take one moment at a time,

Just relax and go with the flow,

For each experience brings you growth,

Even if it may seem to be quite tough,

We can't always have the smooth,

We also have to take the rough,

Often what may seem too hard to change,

Brings the best outcome,

Have a little faith and you will see,

Just what you can become,

As every caterpillar has his day,

To transform into the most beautiful butterfly,

Change is an important part of life,

It ensures that life doesn't just pass you by...

For Gillie Childs

THEY'RE JUST A PERSON LIKE YOU

Some may have a different skin than yours,
Is that any reason to begin wars?
THEY'RE JUST A PERSON LIKE YOU ...

Some have different beliefs inside,
Should that be a reason for them to feel like they must hide?
THEY'RE JUST A PERSON LIKE YOU ...

Some may have a disability,
But maybe it's there to teach something to you and me?
THEY'RE JUST A PERSON LIKE YOU ...

Some may be old and advanced in their years,
But they still feel the same as you inside, and cry the same tears
THEY'RE JUST A PERSON LIKE YOU ...

Some may like women, some may like men,
Some may like both, so what? Is that a crime then?
THEY'RE JUST A PERSON LIKE YOU ...

There are many reasons why we are quick to judge,
Why we don't see beneath the surface, or hold a grudge,

But one thing's for sure, we all come from the same stardust above,
We are all the same inside...we are all LOVE

For Myrna Organ

THE SNOWFLAKE FAIRY

This morning as I looked outside,

There was a lovely sight to behold,

The Snowflake fairy had visited in the night,

And left her icy signature oh so cold,

She had danced around the garden,

Leaving her white powder on the trees,

She left her ice crystals for me to marvel at,

In my garden of deep freeze,

A dusting of icing sugar flakes,

Lay upon the ground,

A sprinkle of glitter strewn everywhere,

As all was still, I heard not one sound,

All except a tiny chime, that is,

As the fairy waved her snowy wand,

And weaved her fabric of ice and snow,

Upon the surface of my little pond,

Thankyou fairy for this magical day,

And for giving us a Winter Wonderland,

May everyone enjoy your wondrous work,

Given lovingly by your fairy hand.

For Beckii Marshall

TEDDY

What would the world be like,

Without a teddy bear to hold?

No furry friend to snuggle up with,

No round tummy for your arms to enfold?

He sits beside your bedside,

And watches over you at night,

He's there when you awaken,

And your dreams give you a fright,

He listens to your sad stories,

His fur soaks up your tears.

You can tell him all about your day,

Your hopes, your dreams, your fears,

But he never sits in judgement,

Just listens carefully,

Always there with a comforting paw,

And a hug that's always free,

He might be a little grubby now,

After many years of being by your side,

But that certainly doesn't mean

His light no longer shines inside,

A teddy's love is like no other,

His cuddles are from the heart,

May you and your beloved teddy

Never ever be apart ...

For Tracy Edley

ANGELS

When I was a little girl,
A light would appear to me at night.
Just before I went to sleep,
To tell me all would be alright,
It had a warm and comforting glow,
That said there's nothing to worry about,
It was my Guardian Angel,
Of that I have no doubt,
She has remained right by my side,
As Guardian Angel's do,
Rest assured my lovely friends,
That you all have one too,
For you are never truly alone,
Even when all seems lost,
She's there with arms outstretched,
When on life's storms you have been tossed,
Sometimes you may feel the feathers,
Of her wings brush by your face,
Or be aware of a special feeling,
Of compassion, humility and grace,
You might feel the gentle ruffle,
Of your hair as she let's you know,
That she's always there no matter what,
Everywhere you go,
So remember all I've told you,
Take comfort in this rhyme,
Your Guardian Angel loves you,
And will be with you til the end of time...

For Catherine Eileen Kozich

SOME PEOPLE CARRY A LIGHT

Some people carry a light in their heart,
And go that extra mile,
To make sure others have all that they can,
They always do it with a smile,
Even when there seems little hope,
Or things aren't looking good,
They keep on going and never give up,
They'd make everything right if they could,
In this world that's run by greed,
They're the light that shines in the dark,
They fight for justice in their own special way,
They really make their mark,
The world would be a better place,
If we would all take their lead,
I am honoured to know such special souls,
The way-showers who plant the seed,
Of truth, love and selflessness,
Of all that is good and right,
Of caring, sharing and humility,
And most of all their guiding light...

For Monica Garthwaite & Neil Geddes-Ward

YOUR FAIRY FRIEND

If you could see what I can see,

A fairy sat on the flower in front of me

With gossamer wings and a sparkling glow

She whispers - I am here you know

I wish that all could see me as you do

It only takes a little bit of practice to

Narrow your eyes and fix your gaze

Until what you see becomes a haze

Now relax yourself and wait a while

No need to be afraid or run a mile

Tiny golden lights will appear

Letting you know that I am here

Keep on looking and you will find

Once you can begin to calm your mind

That you remember me from years ago

Before you had to get big and grow

When you were a child and we played together

Hide and seek in amongst the heather

Collecting dew for a fairy tea

Making daisy chains just you and me

Dancing round a toadstool fairy ring

Listening to the songs the flowers sing

Oh wont you wake up and remember your fairy friend

When you were sad I helped your heart to mend

I'm still here, please don't forget

To find me again there's still time yet

Open your heart and quieten your thoughts

So once again we may get up to all sorts

Hope to see you soon, I'm now off to tend,

My flowers and plants....love your fairy friend...

For Wendy Farrell

THE CHILD INSIDE

Do you remember all my lovely friends

When you were oh so small?

The days seemed to go on forever

And you did not know how it was to be tall

Everything was full of magic

It was to be found everywhere you went

Can you remember using blankets

To make a den or a tent?

When you enjoyed the fact it was raining

And you felt the raindrops on your face

Everything was cool and awesome

And your best friend thought you were ace!

Hide and seek in the woods

Tearing round on your bike

Using your imagination

To pretend you were whoever you liked

Painting, getting messy

Muddy from splashing in puddles

Bedtime stories before going to sleep

And lots of Mummy cuddles

That child is still within you now

Waiting to play again

Find that feeling inside your heart

All you need do is remember when ...

For Kate Hayward

THE LITTLE ELF

One day in the forest

I was surprised to see

A little elf on a toadstool

Smiling at me

He said I'll give you one wish

As you have been good

Then I was surrounded by fairy dust

Right where I stood

Now let me tell you

What my wish was for

It was for all reading this

To be happy and healthy forever more...

For Graham Newton

CHILDREN

What treasures are our children

Treat them accordingly

Each one has a talent to be nurtured

They're a gift to humanity

How can we teach them respect

If they don't receive it from us

They are all unique individuals

The school system doesn't work half the time because...

Children are treated like sheep

They must all do the same thing at the same time

There's no time given to find out what their gifts are

It really is such a crime

Young people need your support

The world's a hard place to navigate

Especially when you're still learning

And if you have other things on your plate

So when you see a child playing up

There's always a reason you see

Give them lots of love and reassurance

And tell them they're valued especially

If I could take each child in the world

And wrap them up in my love

I would tell them they're so special

And a blessing from up above...

For Moira Landry & Mindy Hanlon

GRATITUDE

Some days we are happy
Some days we are sad
But every day's a different day
And of that I'm very glad
Whatever's coming next
Always in your heart have gratitude
Good things will follow and come your way
If you keep a thankful attitude
Next to the energy of Love
Gratitude is an energy oh so high
Count your blessings every day
For the things money just can't buy
The people in your life
The roof over your head
Don't get caught up in the negatives
Be grateful for what you have instead
For as you send your thanks
And not worry about 'lack'
More things to be grateful for
Will boomerang right back
So today I want to say
Thankyou to all of you
For loving and supporting me
In whatever I may do
I'm grateful for all the special people
That have been sent my way
Think about what you have to be thankful for
In the present- the gift of today...

For Tracey Pearson

THE LITTLE LEAF

The little leaf bathed in the sunshine
As he lay upon the stony ground
He gazed up in to the starry sky at night
And watched as life went on all around
He saw children playing in the park
And lovers walking hand in hand
Birds soaring up on high above
Seasons changing across the land
He wondered what it would be like
To be flying, wild and free
To see all the world beneath him
And to wander endlessly
He wanted to go on an adventure
To see the wonders of the world
To feel all the things that others did
Let his potential be unfurled
After all his dreaming
A miracle occurred
The wind came along and took him high
He flew just like a bird
His heart was filled with love
For the sights he saw below
For all his new discoveries
And all the things the wind did show
To this day he floats upon the wind
Experiencing and learning as he goes
We are all like leaves upon the wind
Having adventures so our heart grows...

For Sharon Richards

ONE MOMENT AT A TIME

They say that time's a healer

They say that time will tell

But really theres no such thing as time

As we should all remember well

All there is, is this very moment

The moment you're reading this

What's gone before is past

Tomorrow does not yet exist

Being present in this moment

Is all you have to think of

What's happening in the here and now

The PRESENT - this gift of love

You can decide to change your future

But you can't change your past

You can't deal with anything that's not in the now

Moments weren't made to last

Time you see, is fluid

You need to try and go with the flow

Don't worry about what's coming tomorrow

You can't deal with what's not here yet, you know

So one moment at a time

Tiny moments are all there are

Give each moment all you have

This attitude will take you far ...

For Rhea Angell

THE OLD MAN'S HANDS

As I looked at the old man's hands

A tear crept up from my soul

As I pondered in his lifetime

What had been their role

Working hard to pay the bills

His hands all dry and raw

When I looked upon his hands this is what I saw

They had wiped tears from many faces

Including often times his own

Cupped his love's face so tenderly

More times than I could have known

Fired bullets at the enemy

In wartime, so long ago

Pulled the trigger reluctantly

Even though they were his foe

Swept children up into the air

As they laughed and cried with joy

Tickling them and ruffling their hair

Mending their favourite toy

Love letters written to his beloved

A hundred times or more

Caring for his precious animal companion

So many times he shook his paw

A soothing touch for those in need

He had no clue how healing this had been

His hands told a thousand tales and more

They were one of the most touching things I've seen...

For Tanya Muttitt

THE ROSE

Imagine how a rose feels
As it emerges from the ground
No longer plunged in darkness
Light sparkling all around

Imagine as it grows tall
Up towards the sky
The view it has of life
As it watches time go by

Imagine then the feeling
When a little bud begins to grow
It peeps out from its petals
And it's little heart begins to glow

Imagine now as it unfurls
It's beauty for all to see
The effect it has upon passers by
As they bathe in it's radiant energy

Imagine how it's fragrant perfume
Touches their very soul
It takes them back in time
To a garden paradise of old

Imagine when the time comes
That the petals begin to fall
It returns happily to the earth
Knowing it touched the hearts of one and all

Imagine then that we're all roses
In this garden we call living
Let the world see the beauty of your heart
And your unique fragrance keep on giving...

For Julie-Anne Brandon

WAKE UP!

Did you know you're all amazing?
There's much more to you than you know
If you could see your true self
You would have no cause to feel low
You are made of stardust
An infinite being of energy
Your body is just a vehicle
You're so much more than what you see
There's no such thing as dying
It's just your energy changing form
So it can experience the next phase of life
It really is the norm

Yes we grieve those who pass on

To other dimensions of their choice

Grieving's a natural process

But some day you'll hear your loved one's voice

They'll tell you that what I'm saying

Is true as true can be

They'll say live your life to the fullest

And be all that you can be

Watch out for those little synchronicities

That tell you you're on the right track

The more that you notice them

The more they'll keep coming back

Look at these beautiful flowers

So vibrant and awake

There are reminders everywhere around us

Saying wake up for goodness sake!

Just like these lovely colours

That's how I see you all

A shining, glowing, unique person

Hear my wake up call...

For Zoe Henry

A RANDOM ACT OF KINDNESS

A random act of kindness

Can change somebody's life

This may sound quite dramatic

But you may just ease somebody's strife

By giving from the heart

This has a ripple effect you see

You might just alter a course of events

For the betterment of humanity

You might think a caring hand upon a shoulder

A hand with someone's heavy load

Is nothing to shout out about

But you'll be on the right and kindest road

So this is what I ask of you

Carry out a random act of kindness somewhere today

No matter how small the kindness is

All concerned will be smiling all the way

For Rachael & Darren Wileman

THE LITTLE BLACK CAT

One dark night at Christmas time

I heard the noise of a tinkly bell

I went outside expecting Santa's sleigh

But what it was I could not tell

After a few days of this same event

I found out what it was

A little black cat with a bell on it's collar

It was very strange because...

For Christmas I'd joked that I'd love a white cat -called 'Angel'

Something I had always dreamed of

But here was a little black one hungry and scared

And in need of comfort and love

She adopted me as her Mummy

And follows me everywhere

She has a special energy

That is really amazing and rare

For when I hold her in my arms

She does something to my heart

She's very comforting and healing

Her big eyes just make you melt and fall apart

Sometimes wishes don't turn out how you expect

But this was meant to be

My little black cat is an Angel after all

I'm so glad she found her way to me

For Kitty Anne

THE WISH

A dream is a wish your heart makes

When you're fast asleep

That's the way the song goes

But it's actually much more deep

A wish is a powerful thought

Full of your hopes and dreams

All of your desires and your goals

Receiving your wish is not as hard as it seems

Write it all down on some paper

As if it's already occurred

Before you release it to the Angels

Make sure you've only used positive words

Then it helps to involve the elements

Earth, fire, water or air

You can burn it or bury it in the ground

Then just let it go without a care

Let the Angels carry your wish

Out in to the Universe on their wings

Just go with the flow and take each day as it comes

And see what your positive intention brings...

For Lisa Brown

GRANDMA

Today as I was walking

Something caught my eye

It was brought to my attention

As I was passing by

In every nearby garden

There were violets growing wild

They reminded me of someone

I knew as a young child

My Grandma wore Oil Of Violets

It was her favourite perfume

And now that I am grown up

Her scent will often fill the room

She always lets me know

When she's around me in this way

She was walking right beside me

When I was out today

I felt her loving presence

That told me all was good

So thankyou Grandma and I love you

I'm happy to see your flowers are in bud

In Memory Of Edith Lucas

THE MOST PRECIOUS GIFT

Time is the most precious gift

If you give your time it can uplift

A lonely heart, a mind in fear

Lend someone a listening ear

It's always time for this or time for that

But someone may need a little chat

Just 5 minutes might be enough

To help someone who's finding life tough

Spend more time with your children and those that you love

Make sure they know its them that you think of

When all your time has passed you by

Don't look back with regret, have no reason to sigh

Let no-one feel on their own, be present, be there,

Give a little time and show you care...

For Will Dewis

IF I LIVED IN THE COUNTRYSIDE

If I lived in the countryside

This is how it would be

I'd sit amongst the trees and flowers

And feel happy, wild and free

In January I'd watch the snow fall

As Ice Fairies scatter crystals all around

In February crocuses and snowdrops

The Fairies entice up from the ground

In March I'd listen to the song of the daffodils

A promise of Spring about to appear

In April, Raindrop Fairies cleanse the land

The gentle rain, a lovely sound to hear

In May the fragrant flowers

Bring their colours, healing to my soul

In June the sunshine would warm my heart

Uplifting in it's role

In July I'd rest under a shady tree

And write endless poems just like this

In August paddle in a bubbling stream

To cool me down ...oh what bliss

September brings the last of the Summer

The Autumn Fairies help harvest all the sheaves

In October I'd dance with the Wind Fairies

And try to catch the twirling leaves

In November I'd watch the starlight

As it twinkles in the clear night sky

And in December bathe in the red and green

As the holly berries catch my eye

This is how I'd live my days

I'd be in Heaven throughout the year

But if I use my imagination

My dream of the countryside's already here...

In Memory Of Bert Lucas

LITTLE SOUL

Remember why you came here
Remember what you chose
Remember what you came to see
Be awakened little rose

Remember who you are
Remember where you're from
Remember what you're here for
Be brave little one

Remember your desires
Remember how fear you would transcend
Remember your intention was happiness
Be love my little friend

Remember you are very special
Remember your inner power
Remember the gifts you brought with you
Be beautiful little flower

Remember your chosen adventures
Remember what was your goal
Remember most of all that you're loved
Just be YOU little soul...

For Ryan Lawton

THE PRINCESS

Once upon a fairytale
The princess was locked up in the tower
Little realising her special worth
Or her own inner power
But in her dreams every night
She fought dragons and foes
She climbed up the beanstalk
To the top of goodness knows
She'd choked on an apple
Given to her by a witch
But no way would she give in
Or be stopped by such a glitch
She'd fought the likes of ugly sisters
And an evil stepmother too
The big bad wolf had tried to eat her
And she'd lost her favourite shoe
From an ugly duckling to a swan
She'd transformed overnight
Now she was ready to share with all
Her inner strength and guiding light
So she kissed the little frog
Who she found by the wayside
He transformed into a prince
And she became his glowing bride
So the moral of my fairytale-
To all you ladies I address
Anything can be overcome
Let forth your power - your Divine Goddess

For Donna Zoe Ann Hinton

THE SUNFLOWER

In the field beyond the stream

A solitary sunflower grew

Alone it stood all day and night

That's all it thought it knew

Then one day it noticed

The light shining down from up above

The sunshine on it's petals

For the first time it felt the warmth of love

It followed and turned to the light each day

And was comforted by it's rays

It knew it had to share this feeling

And teach others the sun's wise ways

So it scattered all it's precious seeds

Helped along by the wind and the breeze

Mother Nature lent a helping hand

And so did the birds and the bees

And soon the field was full of flowers

Not just sunflowers though

All colours, shapes and sizes

There was room for all to grow

And so the cycle keeps on going

As more flowers blossom and turn towards the light

The field has no room for shadows

Never has there been a more beautiful sight...

For Geraldine Duran

BLUEBELL WOODS

Once upon a Springtime

I came across a place

Where magic floated on the air

And the energy was one of grace

A sea of blue stretched out before

Inviting me to take a swim

And dive into it's perfumed depths

So I indulged in my little whim

As I lay down upon the earth

The flowers bowed their heads to me

Acknowledging my presence there

Then I was lost in my reverie

Their fragrance lifted up my soul

Their colours healing too

What a gift they bestowed on me

That wondrous mass of blue

I wondered how the fairies made

Such perfect little blooms

Did they sit and wave their magic wands

Whilst sitting on mushrooms?

And where did the perfume come from

That filled the air with Heavenly scent

It seemed like an eternity

That I lay indulging in my heart's content

But when time came to return to the world

A small tear from my face fell

For I would have to wait another year

Til I could once more be in the land of Bluebell.

For Colin Wathen

HAPPY MOTHERS DAY!

H onouring all the Mums, Grandmas and Aunties today

A nd sending our appreciation to you

P lease enjoy your special day

P recious is the job that you do

Y our loving ways help the world go round

M ums are a gift to us all

O ur hearts go out to you today and always

T o the ones that help us stand tall

H eaven sends us all an Angel

E verytime a Mum is born

R oses of the sweetest kind, and the

S unshine that comes with each new dawn

D on't take your Mum for granted

A lways be there for her too

Y ou'll never have another one

Love to all Mum's and a great big thankyou

For Linda Mac

THE BABBLING BROOK

Over ancient stones

The water gurgled and shook

As I sat on the grassy bank

Mesmerised by the babbling brook

Never stopping, always flowing

Not worrying where to or from

We would all do well to take this approach

Just keep going and carry on

Let your energy be like the water

Refreshing all who cross your path

Let your giggles bubble to the surface

And make everyone you meet laugh!

Just like the ancient rocks within the brook

Who have seen many things in their time

Your soul has had many experiences

Not only in this lifetime

Just as the constant flow of water

Shapes the rocks and stones

Each experience has shaped who you are today

They are the seeds that you have sewn

Listen carefully to flowing water

And what it has to say to you

For water carries wise, ancient memories

There's even more to water than this too

In fact there's more to everything around us

If we just think outside the box

Even just sitting by a babbling brook

Nature does her magic, and secrets she unlocks...

For Randi Ansted-Guyer

THE MORNING ANGEL

She casts her warm enchanting smile
Across vast oceans, land and sea
Good morning says her radiant glow
As her sunshine reaches through the window to me

The birds answer with their Dawn Chorus
So happy that she is here once more
The animals stir and bathe in her rays
Making their little hearts soar

The gift of life she bestows
On tiny seedlings deep beneath the ground
Her sunbeams dance across the Earth
Scattering goodness all around

Like a blanket she lays upon the ground
Her sparkling morning dew
Most of us are fast asleep
While her work is carried through

Her arms outstretched she hugs us all
With her tender warmth and care
Good day to each and everyone
May your day pass without a care...

For Bonnie Oles

FAIRY BEARYS LOVE TO KNIT AND SEW

Fairy Bearys love to knit and sew

And make pretty clothes for all their friends

They weave love into each perfect stitch they make

So as well as holes, hearts they also mend

Using gossamer and morning dew

Soft petals and dandelion clocks

They will make whatever is required

Even a pair of toadstool patterned socks

For Sandra Bean

THIS JOLLY GNOME

Once upon a time
This jolly gnome appeared to me
He was very ancient
And as kind as kind could be
Making me laugh with his funny ways
And lifting me up with his smile
He stood at my bedside
Talking of crystals and caves for a while
He is one of a few little folk
Who have appeared to me recently
They wish me to tell you all about them
And bring you closer to their world you see
For each and every one of us
Has a Nature Spirit guide
But years ago they retreated
Man caused them to go and hide
Now is the time for them
To come back into our lives
They have much wisdom to impart
And each little fairy soul strives
To show you the beauty in nature
And to live in harmony
How to be happy and joyful
Will you take this magical journey with me?

For Patrick Kavanagh

FAIRY BEARY AND RABBITINA

Fairy Beary and Rabbitina
Were having a cupcake tea
With a little acorn teapot and cups
They chatted merrily
About how Mr Bumble's honey
Made the most delicious treats
It really was quite clever
His honey making quite a feat
They talked of their friend Mr Gnome
And his fishing expedition downstream
They discussed the lovely Bluebell Woods
Their perfume was like a dream
They sat there passing a happy hour
Until the dandelion clock said time was up
But not before they had eaten every last crumb
And emptied their acorn cups

For Dianne Hall Tew

ONE DAY IN THE FOREST

One day in the forest

I was surprised to see

A little elf on a toadstool

Smiling at me

He said I'll give you one wish

As you have been good

Then I was surrounded by fairy dust

Right where I stood

Now let me tell you

What my wish was for

It was for all reading this

To be happy and healthy forever more...

For Kelly - Lou Faye

WHEN WE LOOK UPON A CHILD'S FACE

When we look upon a child's face

We see a little Angel full of grace

But remember we were all children one upon a time

So what if we are no longer in our prime?

We still have the heart of that child inside

Set your inner child free - don't let it hide

And when on an adult's face you look upon

Remember that child- for it's not gone

If we were to view each other as we do a child

Our attitude would be meek and mild

And what a nicer world it would be

If we remembered that child in you and me....

For Evi Diamond

INTENTION

If it all fell apart at the seams

If you did not quite achieve your dreams

If the end of the world it seems

Then please consider this...

If you did your personal best at the time - but...

If it was an uphill climb

If you feel to fail was a crime

Then it all comes down to INTENTION - because...

If you have done all you could

If you have done everything you should

If you have acted for the greater good

Then you can do no more.FULL STOP.

For Christa Van Vliet

SUNSHINE

The sunshine's smiling on the Earth today

Shining down love and warmth with each sparkling ray

Sunbeams dance and dapple spotlights on the ground

Seeking out all life waiting to be found

Healing cells with every glowing touch

Helping everything to grow, for us all it does so much

Thankyou sunshine for wrapping your golden arms around us,

each and every one

When dark clouds appear we miss you when you're gone

But without the dark we would not appreciate the light

Or be glad to greet the day after the longest night

So be happy that there's sunshine lighting up your day

Even if only a glimmer through the clouds is all that can find it's way

Eventually the clouds will break, and the sun will make it's way to you

But you can always have sunshine in your heart,

no matter what you do ....

In Memory Of Bernice Steane

THROUGH THE EYES OF A FOX

Being chased by dogs, and men on horseback brandishing guns
Would a human enjoy that, would he find it fun?

Yes I am what you term an 'animal', but I'm also a sentient being
with a soul
A different kind of creature than you, but while on Earth I have my role

As does every other being sharing life on this sphere for a while
We each bring our unique energies, EVERY life is worthwhile

Each precious soul, be it animal or human, is here to experience,
evolve and grow
What gives a human the right to cut short that spiritual flow?

Who is the real animal - the fox or the man?
But I forgive the human, just like an animal can

For an animal loves unconditionally
A big part animals play, is teaching unconditional love
to set human's free

So when in my last moments of Earthly life,
I won't be thinking ill of those who made my ending one of strife

Instead I'll look up into the eyes of the one who comes to
collect my body
And hope he sees the compassion for him and forgiveness in me

Then just maybe my mission will have been one of success
If a spark of compassion grows in his heart, and his aggression
becomes less

There's always a bigger picture, two sides of the coin
One day humans alongside animals, in unconditional love will join...

For Juliet Martyn

THE FAIRY WEDDING

One Midsummers Eve, sat on the forest floor

I was surprised to see an open door

Surprising because it opened in the trunk of a tree

And fairy light twinkled out at me

Then there was movement emerging through the door

As I caught my breath and watched in awe

For a wedding party, a bride and groom

Stepped out amongst the leaves and blooms

The bride, a fairy with golden hair

The groom, an elf so tall and fair

And then the assortment of guests- brownies, pixies and gnomes

Who had ventured out of their forest homes

To witness the union of these ethereal creatures

With such delicate, dainty and tiny features

The bride in her dress of gossamer silk

Her skin shone like moonlight and was as white as milk

The groom in his forest inspired attire

He had on his best oak leaf suit and his eyes sparkled like fire

The happy procession glided along the root of the tree

Which was leaf-lined and decked out in fairy finery

Awaiting their presence at the far end

Were further guests who'd been asked to attend

Along with an ancient one who stood proud with his staff

He put everyone at ease by making them laugh!

And conducted the beautiful rose petal filled ceremony

While later that night the forest was alive with their revelry

The next day as people walked their dogs by that spot

They would not have noticed the tiny, still steaming cooking pot

Left by the revellers, that was the only evidence left behind

But I will always carry that extraordinary privilege

to have been there in my mind

For Fee Wilcox

WITH LEAVES FOR MY CEILING

With leaves for my ceiling

And grass beneath my feet

With flowers like jewels around me

And sunshine for my heat

With birds singing for my music

And wind blowing softly through the trees

With the gentle calming waterfall

That helps my soul to ease

With the healing blue of the sky

And the clouds that float along

With the animals resting in the shade

I could sit here all day long

For George Geary

ANGEL MAGIC

When you call upon the help of an Angel
It may arrive in an unexpected form
A white feather left to make their presence known
A silver lined cloud at the end of a storm

A hand upon your shoulder
From a stranger with a kind smile
A phone call or a letter
From a friend you've not seen in a while

A kindness that touches your soul
And brings to your eyes a tear
A feeling of peace and tranquility
That banishes all of your fear

A rose that exudes a perfume
Much stronger than all the rest
A ray of sunshine that warms your heart
When life has put you to the test

When an Angel has touched you
I can assure you, you will know
Take that love out into the world
And spread Angel magic wherever you go...

For Christine Ryan

SOMEWHERE HIGH UP IN A TREE

Somewhere high up in a tree

Bird-song filled the air

Thankful for help tidying up the nest

Mummy bird chirped to each little Gnome Bear

With sunny smiles and a loving heart

The Gnome Bears were happy in their task

Careful not to disturb the eggs

Mummy bird kindly asked

But the Gnome Bears were oh so gentle

As careful as can be

For their hearts were as a light as a feather

It was a lovely sight to see

For Louloute & Beatrice

KEEP YOUR MUMMY IN YOUR HEART

Keep your Mummy in your heart

Always greet her with arms open wide

For you have had the privilege

To hear her heartbeat from the inside....

For Mary Steed

THROUGH THE EYE OF A NEEDLE

Do you feel like you're being squeezed through the eye of a needle?
Do you feel like you're in the eye of the storm?
Just remember that after each dark and stormy night
Morning brings sunshine so warm

The Earth is under much pressure
Change is happening to humanity as a whole
Change is occurring everywhere
For each and every beautiful soul

Know that all is as it should be
We are all positioned in place
The energies affecting every single one of us
Are gathering a magical pace

So sail through the eye of the needle
And ride within the storm's eye
For once we are through to the other side
Our consciousness will have lifted so high

As if attached to a million butterflies
Our light hearts will surely lift
And we will know that every experience we have encountered
Was a truly miraculous gift...

For Mandi Arnold

GRACE

Mummy Bear said one evening at tea

Let us give our thanks and say Grace

But Little Bear had already started to eat his soup

And was filling his dear little face!

Who is this Grace who we thank every time?

Little bear frowned and said

Why doesn't she come round here for tea?

Then we can thank her in person instead

For Emily Ashleigh

BLACKBERRIES

The little gnome bears hid amongst the leaves

Waiting til all was quiet and still

So they could pick the berries and have a feast

But first they had to roll them downhill

Once at the bottom they were covered in juice

Blackberry covered fur and paws

So they all sat down on the cool green grass

And drank all the juice with some straws

For Cynthia Frewin

THE MAGICAL OAK

Walking through the forest

One magical Autumn day

I heard the leaves calling to me

Please come and walk this way

They rustled and swirled

Dancing around my feet

And formed a golden pathway

Beckoning me towards who I should meet

Before me stood a majestic sight

A beautiful ancient oak

Home of a myriad number of Earthly creatures

Along with all kinds of fairy folk

It's branches bowed before me

And welcomed me to sit down

As it told me tales of long ago

All around me it's acorn gown

It spoke to me through the rustle of it's leaves

And images formed in my mind

It possessed a wisdom I had not known before

And it's words were gentle and kind

A thousand glowing Nature Spirits

Were witness to it's tale

Nymphs, fairies, elves and gnomes

Listened intently to all that it regaled

I cannot begin to put into words

The message imparted to me

But it soothed my soul, healed my heart

And set my Spirit free

So if you should walk amongst the trees

And come across a magical oak

Spend some time within it's presence

And take heed of what it spoke

For Ragnhildur Johnsdottir

BUBBLES OF LOVE

May bubbles of love blow far and wide today

Around the world, all the way

To touch each heart they happen upon

May they uplift each and every one

Cleansing sorrow, loss and pain

Let there be sunshine where there is rain

Their rainbow colours heal each soul

Mending hearts to make them whole

Floating, I send them to you on the breeze

Up where the clouds are, and over tops of trees

They will seek you out wherever you are

Whether you are near or whether you are far

So when yours goes pop and out pours the love

Know that it was Heaven sent from above

May you be wrapped in it's rainbow of joy for ever more

May you never see the strife and sorrow of fighting and war

May these iridescent orbs rid war from the land

And allow all those fighting to disengage and disband

May they too be touched by a bubble of love and light

Enabling them to see the error of their plight

There are enough bubbles to touch one and all

If you will just imagine with me, and watch as everywhere they softly fall...

For Jackie Dean

HAVE SANTA'S ELVES BEEN TO FETCH YOUR LIST YET?

Have Santa's Elves been yet, to fetch your list?

Did they come one frosty night?

Did they leave a trail of Elf dust?

And then disappear out of sight?

If you wrote your most heartfelt wishes,

You can be sure that Santa will take note,

His 'Ho Ho Ho' will ring out loud and clear,

If you remembered others in all that you wrote...

For Santa, being the oldest Elf of all,

Has a heart even bigger than his tummy,

He says it's good to think of others too,

Your friends, your family and of course Mummy.

So if your list is still to be written,

And you ask for that new dolly, a bike, a car,

Save a little space to make a wish for someone else too

Your kind thought will take you far.....

For Michelle Bradley & Sam

THE MAGICAL BOOK

Somewhere underneath the dust and clutter

If you will take a little time to look

I lie waiting for you to find me again

And remember me - your favourite childhood book

Oh what adventures we used to have

Each time you turned my pages

Fairies, witches, cowboys and indians

Dragons and giants from other ages

My paper soaked up your salty tears

When by the sadness of my words you were overcame

I would take pleasure in your laughter at my funny parts

Each time your love for my stories was the same

Your face lit up each time you picked me up

Your tiny hands held me so tight

With your torch way after bedtime

You read me long into the night

Now I sit and wait for you
So I can bring you pleasure one more time
You and I sat together by the fireside
Would surely be sublime

For I would open up your heart once more
So you could find your inner child again
And spread the magic of my words
To inspire you to pick up your pen

And weave your own unique story
Paint your own pictures too
I have so much more I'd like to give
Come and find me again won't you...

For Stewart Bint

I REALLY MISS YOU DAD

I really miss you Dad
You were my comfort and my guide
To be known as your daughter
I can take the greatest of pride

You're now the sparkle in each raindrop
The golden glow in each sunbeam
You're in the gently blowing breeze
The flowing water in every stream

You're in the trees as they softly whisper
The leaves rustling on the ground
In every lovely flower petal
Your loving Spirit can be found

In the morning chorus of the birdsong
In the rainbow's colours up on high
In every cloud floating silently
Across the deep blue sky

Dad, you loved all of Nature
And now of all those beautiful things you are a part
But there's one place I know for sure you'll always be
And that is in my heart

In Memory Of John Lucas

DAD

Today as you were walking

Did you think it was me that you saw?

In the shapes up in the clouds above

As you gazed at them in awe?

Did you think you saw me leaning

Against that old oak tree?

Smiling proudly as you passed by

Yes my darling, it was me

And as that robin sang so beautifully

Did you think I sent it just for you?

Or when the sunshine warmed your skin

Did you think I had a hand in that too?

Was that me in the wil-o-the-wisp of leaves

That suddenly swirled on the ground?

Yes you're right on every count

For with you, I am all around

I am the in the breeze that cools you

On a Summer's day

I am in the flowers that bring you beauty

I am with you all the way

For in life I gave you all the love

And protection a Dad could give

I am still with you my darling, in everything

For as long as on the Earth you shall live...

For Helen Goodman

YOU LEFT YOUR MARK ON THE WORLD DAD

You left your mark on the world Dad

You left it in my heart

Your kindness shone above all others Dad

Where do I even start?

You left your mark on the world Dad

A gentleman through and through

You touched all our lives with your love Dad

And you put all of us before you

You left your mark on the world Dad

Which shows in every falling tear

You were a totally amazing Dad, Dad

If only you were still here...

For Dawn, Eric, Katie & Harry

CAKE MIX!

While I was mixing a cake just now
I thought about the mixture in the bowl
That some of it won't make the cake tin
But that doesn't mean it's not got it's own role

It reminded me of some special people
Who think they're not good enough to make the grade
I hope this message will warm your hearts
And all of your doubts will fade

The mixture left inside the bowl
May not have made it into the tin
But to many the mixture tastes better than the actual cake
It usually makes everyone grin

So in the same way, some people
May think they've not got what it takes
But just like the mixture left around the bowl
You're often nicer than the nicest of cakes!

In Memory of Ida and Sid Kavanagh

SENDING OUT A MILLION HEARTS

Sending out a million hearts today,

Around the world, all the way,

To all my friends and those in need,

I hope my words of love will sew a seed,

And you'll want to pass on this good energy,

To those in your thoughts and all that you see,

The world can become a better place, one thought at a time,

So I start with YOU, the person reading my rhyme,

I send you my love and a challenge to you,

Make a positive change today, with something you say or do,

You'll be surprised how good it will make you feel,

Because positive thoughts have the power to heal,

Lots of love and blessings to you out there,

I write you these words because about you I care...

For Lyn, Garry, Luke & Daniel

SENDING OUT ANGELS

Sending out Angels today to watch over all of you

Everywhere you go and in everything you do

Healing your hearts and keeping you safe

All will be well, just gotta have a little FAITH...

For Bob Ames

COMFORT AT CHRISTMAS

In his crystal cave the little gnome dwells

Awaiting the sound of Santa's sleigh bells

Magic in the air, and Christmas Spirit in his heart

He knows that for some, Christmas means being apart

From loved ones and family, from those that mean the most

He sends his love to you all through this little rhyming post

The magic of the crystal he sends to each and every aching heart

Comfort and reassurance it's radiance imparts

To one and all, if this little poem strikes a note

May all the love he sends to you, keep your heart and soul afloat

For Michelle & Graham Green

HAPPY NEW YEAR!

May the Fairies weave LOVE throughout all your days,

May they make your life MAGICAL in their wondrous ways,

May this be the year that you rise and SOAR,

May you all walk through a new, open and shining DOOR,

May Angels and Fairies guide you on your life's PATH,

May they bring you joy and fun, and make you LAUGH!

May they bring to you all HEAVEN ON EARTH,

May all this be yours as the NEW YEAR births.....

For Karen Twigg

SENDING A LITTLE MAGIC

Sending a little magic and sparkle your way,

May your wishes come true throughout the day,

If it can be imagined, then it can come true,

Dream the biggest dream that it's possible to...

In Memory Of Fred & Edna Healey

I WOKE UP FEELING FAIRY-FIED

I woke up feeling fairy-fied,

My heart all of a flutter,

I know that some will read my poem,

And think that I'm a nutter! :)

That may be so, but I just want to share,

My open- heartedness with all of you,

To tell you - find your inner child,

And put love in all you do,

I want to touch your heart with my fairy wand,

I want to take away all your pain,

I want to tell you that all will be ok,

If all you try seems to be in vain,

I'm always here no matter what,

If you need help just call to me,

I may be a nutter like you think,

But I'm with you totally!

For Sally Louise Thomas

FAIRY NUFF

There once was a fairy
Who's name was Nuff
She looked very dainty
But she was very tough

Her wings took her on adventures
Around the world far and wide
In fact throughout the Universe
She flew on the cosmic tide

The sights that she saw
Were a wonder to behold
The stories that she has
Are begging to be told

But one thing that she saw
No matter where she went
Is that love underlies all
It's truly Heaven sent

It's an energy
That pervades all things
The stars and the planets
Right down to a butterflies wings

Everywhere she went
She saw a rainbow of hope
It's colours shining down
Like a love kaleidoscope

How many times in conversation
Do we say it's 'fair enough' (Fairy Nuff)
Well just remember when you hear it
Love is everywhere...
There's loads of the stuff!

For Amy Harrison

THE YOU YOU'LL BE TOMORROW

The you you'll be tomorrow
Is not the you you are today
You're a completely different you
Than the one you were yesterday!

Millions of your cells die every second
50 million by the time you read this
Some of your cells are replaced with brand new ones
In the time it takes for a sweet kiss

It's not just your physical body
That's being constantly created anew
Your whole life is being created
By the thoughts that occur to you

You're creating your reality each moment
It doesn't just happen to you
That's why there are endless possibilities
So be mindful in all that you do

Upon waking tomorrow morning
The first thing you must do is to smile
By exuding that positive energy
You'll have a much better day by a mile

Then put love into all of your actions
And x100 it will boomerang back
Remember your thoughts are an energy
Do this and you're on the right track...

For Wendy Sheard

PASSING

Today I spoke to someone
And this is what she said
My time is near for passing on
But please don't think of me as 'dead'

She asked me to impart her message
And bring comfort to all I can
To those of you who are grieving a loss
I'm just going home - she began

I'm made of an energy that just keeps on going
No matter what form I may take
Please don't think of me as gone
Because somewhere I'll be wide awake!

Like a snake I'll shed my body
And leave that part of me behind
But I'll be free of all illness and worry
No longer in my body confined

I am needed elsewhere now
It's time for me to go
But before I leave this Earthly life
There's something I want you to know...

Make each moment matter
For each lifetime is gone in the blink of an eye
Follow your heart and your dreams
Don't wait until you pass over to let your Spirit fly

To shed tears for me is natural
To grieve your loss is normal too
But please don't think that's the end of me
To say it's the next phase of my journey is true

I'm going on an adventure
She told me as her eyes softly closed
Time stood still in that moment
As I watched her Spirit as it rose

Like a thousand stars on a moonlit night
The most beautiful thing I have seen
Her Spirit shone brightly as it left the Earth
While her body lay calm and serene

I know I'll be talking to her later
When she tells me what adventures she's had
And to know I've told you her story
She'll be so very happy and glad

For in the words of the song - 'The Heart Does Go On'
It can never fade or die
Fill your heart with the utmost love
All the things that money can't buy

Because that's all you can take with you
When the next part of your journey calls
And remember Spirit (energy) is everywhere
From trees and flowers, to waterfalls

It's what animates our bodies
When we experience being human for a while
And knowing all these things I'm saying to you
Is why my lady left with a smile...

Sybil & Martin Moore and In Memory Of Nicola Moore

TO ALL MY LITTLE SPARKLES

Making things today with Fairy Dust

It made me think of all of you

Each one of you is a tiny sparkle of life

Reflecting light in all you say and do

You all have different and unique facets

Showing all your colours and shades

Even when in darkness

Your light never dulls or fades

Each tiny little sparkle

Shines so brightly in it's own right

But look what happens when you all come together

Like a million stars on a beautiful night

So all my lovely little sparkles

Imagine what together you could do

Your light would outshine any darkness in the world

And beam out throughout the Universe too.

For Sharon, Karl, Kasey & Cody

AN ENCOUNTER IN THE FOREST

Can you see the Fairies having their meeting?

Sitting on the stones waving to you their greeting?

The stones themselves recording all that was spoken

The Fairies hoping that your senses have awoken

And as light as a feather you feel their love

That holds your heart like a gossamer glove

For Tracey Knights

MY FRIEND – THE TREE

I sat upon a grassy knoll

While my friend imparted his wisdom to me

My friend though was no ordinary one

For my friend, in fact was a tree

He eased my cares and listened

Like every human should

There are more than enough tree friends to go around

If you should wander in forest or wood

He sheltered me from the raging storm

And shared his fruits lovingly

He kept me cool in the shade of his leaves

Such a friend is rare, I'm sure you'll agree

He told me how he strived

To reach his branches towards the light

How he provided warmth and shelter

To many creatures in the coldness of night

How he helped to cleanse the air

So we could breathe it in safely

And how his blossoms in Springtime

Gave us a wondrous sight to see

Please send my plea to all humans - he said

And give them a message from me

On behalf of my tree friends everywhere

We await your friendship patiently

For Caroline Ackermann

EVEN THE STARS COME DOWN TO EARTH TO BATHE

Even the stars come down to Earth to bathe

In the sparkling ocean

The salty waves lap softly

More healing than any Earthly potion.

For Gill Hickey

LIGHT

Standing in the light

Reflecting on my life

I pondered, why if light was all around me

Why sometimes I must endure darkness and strife

Then I heard a voice inside me

Speaking gently from within

It told me darkness was an illusion

There was no such thing as sin

All that really exists is LOVE

The rest is all a dream

You are here to find your way back to what is real

All that glitters is not gold, or what it may seem

I pondered these words, that came from my soul

And what exactly they might mean

As I did so, the voice spoke once again...

YOU ARE THE LIGHT and have always been ...

For Magdalena Korytkowska

LITTLE SIGNS

Little signs are left in Nature

From the little folk, to reveal

And act as reminders of all the LOVE in the world

And how that LOVE can heal

In the tiniest grain of sand

In the bark of a tree

In the billowing clouds up on high

All are expressions of Universal LOVE for us all to see

When the Fairies weave their magic

Into matter with their LOVE

Atoms are rearranged

To form these hearts - symbols from above

Look out for these Nature messages today

If you see one, it's just for you

To tell you how very loved you are

Now go and share it with the whole world too...

For Maria Collin

LIFE AND LIGHT WILL ALWAYS FIND A WAY

With all the events in the world today
I thought I would write these few words
Everyone has their own point of view
But everyone deserves to be heard

It's easy to judge a situation or someone
When the facts are not all present
It's also easy to get something wrong
When on truth you are dependant

We should all respect each other's views
Our choices and our thoughts
We should all respect each other - full stop.
This is what's wrong with the world - when each other we don't support

A choice has been made, what's done is done
There is a reason it's gone this way
Whatever will be, is supposed to be
Let's move forward TOGETHER from today

Now we have to make the best of what we have
Our country and our people need us to unite
Let's be positive and work as ONE
Because NOTHING will work if we fight

One thing is for sure, and that is this

We are all in this TOGETHER come what may

And whatever our collective tomorrow brings

Life and Light will always find a way...

For David Mayne

IF I LIVED IN THE FOREST

If I lived in the forest
I'd live in a toadstool house
I'd spend my days talking to the trees
Then curl up inside at night like a wee mouse

I'd take tea with Mrs Rabbit
And have lunch with Mr Fox
Then we would play race the seed
With fluffy white dandelion clocks

On a moonlit Summer's night
We'd gaze upon the stars
And roast marshmallows on the fire
Whilst discussing Jupiter and Mars

If all of this sounds like nonsense
Then I don't really care
For it's now time to visit Fairyland
With my good friend Mr Hare

For Ilia Clotilde Orellana Espinoza

CLOUDLAND

In my dreams I float above

The clouds that drift on high

Another land awaits me

Created by the Fairies of the sky

Into the 'cotton wool' clouds

Their Fairy dust they weave

So that when us humans might look up

Shapes are seen within them - which help us to believe...

That Magic exists within all things

There's so much more than meets the eye

Look past the material world around you

A good place to start - the clouds that glide on by

For this is how it works-

Your thoughts are creating your reality

So to test this theory out

Just think of something - and in the clouds it's shape shall be

In the meantime I will enjoy

My time resting in Cloudland

In the land of softness and sparkle

Created by the Fairies own fair hand...

For Pat Mallabone

THE GATEWAY

WE are standing on the threshold

Waiting at the gate

A Golden new era awaits us

Take my hand, don't hesitate

A leap of faith is required here

To make the transition from old to new

All we have to do is trust

And follow Love, and what is true

So come with me down the Fairy path

I'll show you a world of peace, with no more hate

Where you can realise your amazing potential

Lets ALL go together, through the magical gate...

For Paul Gardner

A MESSAGE FROM YOUR GUARDIAN ANGEL

Come and walk the Earth with me
For this little while you're here
Let me enfold you in my wings
Whenever there is strife or fear

I am with you even before you arrive
In this world that you call home
I hold your hand and guide you on life's path
Wherever you choose to roam

You are never alone in this world
For I am forever by your side
Talk to me, release your stress and strain
In me you can confide

Sometimes you may feel my touch
Or hear my whisper on the breeze
My messages may come in surprising ways
Such as in the movement of the trees

Alone at night when you are troubled
And lying in the dark
My light shines right beside you
Like a brilliant golden spark

As a child you may remember
Chatting happily to me
About all the things you would do in life
And all the things you were going to be

So I stand with you and remind you
Of all that is possible for you to achieve
I have every faith in your abilities
In yourself you must believe

Remember, my job is to love you
Right from before your birth
I will always pick you up if you should fall
Until together, hand in hand we leave the Earth...

For Sue Baker

WHAT'S A BIRTHDAY LIKE IN HEAVEN DAD?

What's a Birthday like in Heaven Dad?

Will you have a birthday tea

Did someone bake you your favourite cake?

Is there room round the table for me?

What's a Birthday like in Heaven Dad?

Did the Angels sing Happy Birthday?

I imagine you were in the most beautiful place

But I wish you were here with us, and you could stay

What's a Birthday like in Heaven Dad?

I can see your bright, smiling face

I'm sure you're making everyone laugh

And you're still a right old case!

What's a Birthday like in Heaven Dad?

A very special present I send to you

It's wrapped up with kisses and cuddles

And all my love forever to you...

For Willow Brown & Family

HEAVEN'S STAIRS

Close your eyes and imagine me
Reaching down to you
All I am is a thought away
In your heart you know that's true

From the top step I sit and watch
Your movements down below
I am so proud to see what you've become
And all you've come to know

If you will quiet your mind for a little while
And meet me half way on Heaven's stairs
I will comfort you with all my love
And soothe away your cares

Just like old times, when I was once on Earth
We can chat the time away
I'll tell you all about life in Heaven
And the wondrous ways I fill each day

As in life below, I am still always here
If you need me any time at all
Just close your eyes and think of me with love
And my heart will hear your call......

For Dawn Vernon

IF I COULD SEND YOU ALL

There is a special place for you
It's somewhere in my heart
For you are always there for me
No matter what distance we are apart

If I could send you all a beautiful scent
It would be the scent of a million roses
For each and every one of you
I'd pick a meadowful of posies

If I could send a sound to you
It would be that of a soothing waterfall
To cleanse your soul and heal your spirit
Sparkling dewdrops for one and all

If I could send you all a wonderful sight
It would be of your families all together and well for ever more
Abundance in every single form
Only joy and peace, no war

If I could send you something good to taste
It would be the creamiest chocolate money can buy
A lorry load for each of you
A never ending lifetime's supply!

If I could give you all a gift to touch
Then it would be something to touch your heart
To let you know you are so very loved
And of my journey I'm so lucky you are a part

For Rebecca, Joe, Hayley & Hollie

FLY LITTLE BUTTERFLY

Fly little butterfly
You've earned your lovely wings
Go out into the world and soar
And see what this new day brings...

For Sue & Mick Storer

AN AUTUMN FAIRY BEAR

It's decidedly Autumn - like today!
The Fairy Bears like to come out and play
With all the leaves that dance in the air
Oh what a time for an Autumn Fairy Bear!

For Sarah Cox

A PUDDLE FULL OF LOVE

Love can be found wherever you look
In every cranny and every nook
In Nature you need not search too far
Love is in every dewdrop and every star
For the Nature Angels create these gifts for you
To show you that you're so very loved, in all you do
So today I send you this puddle full of Love
To remind you of how much you are ALWAYS thought of ...

For Tammy Rayner

THE LITTLE FEATHER

One day in my bedroom
I happened upon a tiny thing
The thing was a tiny feather
I also heard a faint 'ting-a-ling'

Puzzled as to what was occurring
I left it upon my drawers
That night as I was drifting off to sleep
I heard faint whispers near my bedroom door

In the darkness I could clearly see
A myriad of twinkling lights
Shining brighter than all the stars up in the sky
It was an enchanting and mystical sight

These lights surrounded miniature figures
With gossamer wings and dresses of lace
There seemed to be a Queen of sorts
Who had the most beautiful Elfin face

I noticed that her lovely gown
Was covered in feathers like the one I had found
I also saw that these tiny folk floated
And their feet did not touch the ground

They did not seem to notice me
As I looked on at them in awe
Nor did I understand what they were doing
Standing by my bedroom door

Just then from within the shadows
Along the skirting board
More small figures started to appear
Into my room hundreds poured

Pondering on this delightful scene
I remembered something from my childhood
One day, once again in my bedroom
On my shelf, a tiny glass tankard stood

Now the Fairy folk began to disappear
From my limited human view
I thought about it all carefully
And in that moment I knew

That there are many wondrous dimensions
Just beyond the naked eye
They overlap with our Earthly world
Sometimes we glimpse them when our energy is high

And if we are very lucky
We may be bestowed a Fairy gift
To remind us of the magic around us
And to give our hearts a lift...

For Tammy Whitehead

THREE LITTLE BEARS

Three little bears curious as could be
One said let's find some honey, come on follow me!

They sniffed and they snuffed, and followed the smell of honey
If you had seen their little snouts it would have looked kind of funny!

Their sniffing was not in vain for they found a buzzing hive
But with hundreds of bees their treasure was alive

So back to Momma bear they ran and asked for her help
For they didn't want those bees to sting them - and make them all yelp!

Momma bear asked the bees politely for a share of their honey
The bees flew aside while Momma Bear shared out the treat so runny

All full and fed to their meadow they returned
Thinking of all the things from Momma Bear they'd learned

All sticky were their whiskers, and their little paws too
But three tired bear cubs were fast asleep before they could clean
off all the goo!

For Richard Backschas

A MESSAGE FROM A
NATURE ANGEL

Have you noticed all the colours
That I paint in Nature just for you
I choose my palette carefully
Making sure I have just the right shade and hue

For I bring my colours to uplift
To bring you joy and happiness
When you see my artwork
Know that you are truly blessed

I paint the daffodils and bluebells
To lift your Spirits in the Spring
Following the cold Winter days
My colours are to make your little hearts sing

In Summertime I give you
Everything I can
All the colours of the rainbow
All the colours known to man

In Autumn a kaleidoscope
Of colours reflected in the trees
All the shades of Earthy brown
As leaves dance upon the breeze

Winter brings the snow
The purity of white
The deepest, darkest blue
On a cold, starry winter night

If I could give you all a rainbow
A full spectrum so beautiful and bright
Then I would do so in a heartbeat
As all colours combined make LIGHT

For Elaine Eshelman Hayes

HOW QUICKLY SOME PEOPLE SOON FORGET

How quickly some people soon forget

Until once more they seek your comforting light

To guide them through their darkest hour

And be their refuge through the night

But in between these times, you're tossed aside

Just like a stone into a stream

Did they really just treat me this way again, I ask myself

Or was it just a dream?

Then I am quick to remind myself

That as long as I've acted in the right way

It's was never really between me and them at all

It was just another test at the end of the day

But when someone gives you their absolute all

And they're there for you no matter what - day or night

Remember like you, they're only human

Be there for them when they need you too - do the thing

that you know to be right...

For Lynne Rebecca Jelonek

THE LITTLE ANGEL (PART 1)

On a cloud, a little Angel sat
Looking down at the world below
She knew what her life's mission was
Now it was time to go

She knew how hard it was going to be
To adjust to the ways of this place
It would be difficult she had no doubt
To become one of the Human Race

She would struggle from day to day she knew
With the challenges daily life would bring
But she would overcome them all
And everyone would hear her heart sing

She would touch every soul she ever met
And send out ripples of love wherever she went
Uplifting those in need of care
Wherever on Earth she was sent

So now it was time to leave her Heavenly cloud
And fly down to her destination on Earth
To spend time with this lady she would come to know as 'Mum'
Before the event of her birth

Once there she listened to the words of love
Spoken about her by 'Mum' and by 'Dad'
And the soft music they played to soothe her
Of the parents she'd chosen she was glad

Soon the day came, when she would make the transition
From her own dimension to this
Time to enter the great big wide world
And leave behind her existence of bliss

She heard a sound as she entered here
It was the sound of her own soft sweet cry
As she remembered for the very last time
The beautiful world of love, she'd just left behind...

For Eden Shields

THE LITTLE ANGEL (PART 2)

Upon entering this strange and unknown world
The Little Angel took her first look around
After her cries for home had quietened a little
Her Mum's heartbeat was the next sound

As she was placed in her Mum's arms
Their two heartbeats were in rhythm as one
Now she forgot all about her home in the Heavens
For her Mum's love was as warm as the sun

Then Dad stepped forward, and she felt his love too
Her protector in this realm called Earth
These two souls were now her family
And she would love them for all she was worth

As she grew, it was clear for all to see
That she had a heart of pure gold
Her light affected all she happened upon
And she was loved by all, young and old

Animals would come to be by her side
She even made the little birds sing
If you were to listen very carefully
All around her you would hear little Angel bells ring

Distant memories of home would stir now and then
And she would feel a loneliness inside
But time spent in Nature and being outdoors
Helped the little Angel take things in her stride

She would talk to the animals and help them
Using flowers, herbs and crystals to heal
She knew exactly what she needed to 'fix' them
By using her ability to feel

Soon more little Angels came to join the family
From their own little clouds up above
The house was filled with Little Angels
Who had all come to share their gift of love...

For Paige Steane

THE LITTLE ANGEL (PART 3)

The little Angel grew up some more
Until it was time for school
As she loved reading her books so much
To learn, she thought it would be so cool

But soon she found it was not all she thought
Her imagination was forbidden to fly
The 'rules' in place were very harsh
And she really couldn't understand why

She was unable to figure out either
Why the adults did not afford the children respect
Why they were all expected to be little sheep, exactly the same
If children misbehaved - what did they expect?

There were many things her heart wished to know
But often there were just facts to learn
Things that would never be needed again
Things that would never be any of her concern

Instead of uplifting, creative tasks
She was often given mundane things to do
Not much of a practical nature was taught
And she was sometimes picked on for being different too

Growing up in this way made her forget even more
Her true home, up above on her cloud
She no longer talked to the fairies and elves
It was frowned upon and not allowed

However, this seemingly negative part of the story I tell
Is not as bad as you might think
All these experiences would shape who she would become
To her inner strength they would all have a link

Ever since before she had been born into this world
Her Guardian Angel had watched over her with love and care
And now as the little Angel became a young lady
You can be sure her presence was still there...

For Anna Richardson

THE LITTLE ANGEL (PART 4)

So now our little Angel
Had reached her teenage years
Growing up she'd faced adversity
And she'd shed many Angel tears

But never did her love waiver
Especially for those more unfortunate souls
She took them under her Angel wings
And with her gentle words she did console

Then one fateful day across a crowded room
She suddenly became aware
Of an energy that felt so familiar
Then she saw him - standing there

Within each other's eyes
The windows of the soul
A thousand lifetimes were revealed
Where each had played out a different role

They'd danced a similar dance
Many times before
And they would surely dance it all again
Of that you can be sure

For there is no higher connection
Than a bond at the level of the soul
Their energies completed each other
And each half made up the whole

Divine timing had worked it's magic
And all had fallen into place
Once more she gazed in awe
At this oh so familiar face

She felt a love inside her
That was so powerful and deep
A little slice of Heaven
That awoke her from her Earthly sleep...

For Holly Kavanagh

THE LITTLE ANGEL (PART 5)

Having now met her soulmate
The one she had been waiting for
This love lifted her to even greater heights
And she saw the goodness in everyone even more

She felt the magic all around her
The deeper meaning within all things
She knew that love was all there really was
It was the glue to which all life clings

Everywhere she roamed in life
An Angelic presence she always felt
In amongst the trees and flowers, rocks and streams
She knew the Nature Angels dwelt

All these things reminded her
Of a place from long ago
A distant memory of somewhere called home
A memory that brought her a warm glow

When her sensitivity
Caused her to feel a little low
She would connect to that Angelic presence
And away her fears would go

To very good use she put her gifts
By helping anyone she could
She awoke them from their Earthly sleep
Then one day her thoughts turned to Motherhood

Many miracles and much magic occurred
For she was gifted with little Angels of her own
She would make sure they knew how loved and cherished they were
And that they would never feel alone

Truly blessed was she to be bestowed with these gifts
Who also touched all they met with their light
She knew that the more little Angels there were in the world
The future was certainly bright...

For Jade Kavanagh

THE LITTLE ANGEL

(PART 6 – THE END, BUT REALLY JUST THE BEGINNING...)

The Little Angel's Little Angels
Grew up to be beautiful souls
They lived by their Mother's example
And fulfilled their pre-destined roles

The Little Angel's Little Angels
Also brought Little Angels into the world, of their own
She was gifted with Grandchildren
Now her life was complete, it was whole

As she looked back on her life
She had no cause for regret or remorse
For all that she had experienced
She knew was for her own growth, of course

She had imparted her wisdom to many
And given all that she could
Though she had made mistakes in her life
Her intentions had always been good

Whatever had transpired between her and others
All had been as it was meant
It had never been between her and them at all
It was all about growth, and was Heaven sent

Now she knew it was time
To return to her little Heavenly cloud
The next part of her eternal journey called
She would leave feeling happy and proud

Her Guardian Angel appeared by her side
Held out her hand and said come with me
She smiled the smile of a million sunbeams
And the Little Angel closed her eyes naturally

A light appeared before her
That radiated warmth and love
Hand in hand with her Guardian Angel
She left this Earth for her little cloud in Heaven above...

For Joy Gamble Spencer